Seville

Text by: Fernando Olmedo

EDICIONES
Aldeasa

Seville

◄ *Streetlamp in the plaza de Santa Cruz.*

From Hispalis to the capital of Andalusia

Seville, the capital of the Autonomous Community of Andalusia and the fourth largest city in Spain, is situated in a valley on the banks of the Guadalquivir River, before from where it meets the Atlantic Ocean. Loaded with history and tradition, bright, monumental, self-assured and hospitable, friendly and passionate, its name is a talisman that arouses and unites many of the charms of the Andalusian region.

Guadalquivir River ▶

From Hispalis to Isbiliya

The roots of Seville date back to the 8th century BC when
it sprung up on a headland of the Guadalquivir estuary.
Although mythology attributes its founding to Hercules,
archeology and the city's primitive name – Hispalis – trace
its origins to the Phoenicians and the legendary Kingdom of
Tartessos, and its fortune to its strategic position at the
intersection of land and sea routes. During Roman times,
Hispalis stood out among the most flourishing trading cen-
ters of the Andalusian province, exporting minerals from the
Sierra Morena Mountains and products – oil, wheat, and
wine – from the fertile Guadalquivir Valley. An importance
that Caesar himself confirmed by giving it the title of
Colonia Iulia Romula. At the same time, the noble city of
Itálica, birthplace of the Emperors Trajan and Hadrian, grew
in the vicinity, its ruins later known as "Old Seville". Under
the Visigoths, the city retained its economic, political, and
cultural importance, giving shelter to notable figures such
as the wise San Isidoro.

Itálica, Roman ruins. Casa del Planetario. ▲

Aerial view of Seville. ▶

Upon the arrival of the Muslims in the year 711, Hispalis discarded its old name in favor of Isbiliya, from which the city's current name is derived. A rival of Cordoba until the fall of the Omeya Caliphs, starting in the 6th century Seville asserted itself over the other cities of al-Andalus, the Islamic Spain, upon becoming the head of the most powerful kingdom of taifas and, in the 7th century the capital of the Andalusian domain of the Moroccan Empire of the Almohads. During the next four-hundred years, it was the most important city on the Peninsula. This age of brilliance, when the city was a meeting point between East and West, left Seville with an extensive walled urban area and some of its most emblematic monuments: the Giralda, the Alcázar, and the Torre del Oro.

The Christian Court and metropolis of the Golden Age

In 1248, Ferdinand III entered Seville, which was to take on the role of Christian bastion against the final redoubt of Spanish Islam, the Kingdom of Granada. Until the fall of Granada, court was habitually held here by monarchs such as San Fernando, Alfonso X the Wise, Peter I, and the Catholic Monarchs. Inhabited by Castilians and Muslims as well as Jewish and foreign minorities, at the end of the Middle Ages it was one of the most dynamic cities in the West, whose prosperity, and the final triumph of Christianity were expressed through the construction of a grandiose Gothic cathedral. Seville's peak was in the 16th and 17th centuries when it held a monopoly on trafficking with the Indies after the discovery of the New World by Columbus in1492. The fleets and galleons that put in at its port, inundated the city with riches, converting it into one of the most booming and cosmopolitan metropolis in Europe, inhabited by a motley population of 150,000 inhabitants. The zenith of this "port and gate to the Indies" in which aristocrats, merchants, religious figures, bureaucrats, artisans, sailors, and scoundrels coexisted, stimulated a brilliant cultural boom: Cervantes, Lope de Vega, Zurbarán and other illustrious figures met in its streets, and Velázquez, Murillo and a legion of other artists were born here. Meanwhile the city was transformed by an infinity of monumental buildings constructed in the Renaissance and Baroque styles. This luster finally dulled in the 17th century under the ravages of disease and the crisis of the Spanish monarchy.

Real Alcázar. Salón de Embajadores (above). ▲
Torre del Oro (below).
Cathedral and the Giralda. ▶

Romantic destination and the capital of Andalusia

Relegated to the functions of a regional capital and agricultural center following its colonial splendor, in the 18th and 19th centuries Seville adopted a more languid and routine rhythm that was only altered by events such as the War of Independence. However, the city's traditional atmosphere, the Southern charm of its people, the exoticism of its Arab heritage and wealth in monuments would soon captivate travelers and artists, shaping Seville's image as a romantic destination and the setting for the universal myths of Don Juan, Fígaro and Carmen.

In the 19th century the city underwent a profound transformation that accelerated into the 20th century. Walls, gates and religious buildings were demolished to make way for plazas (squares) and avenues. Residential areas were laid out, the Santa Cruz district and the parque (park) María Luisa were revamped, and the city was subjected to an ambitious project that would give its growth direction, the Latin American Expo of 1929, which left a permanent mark on its physiognomy. The definitive modernization of the city was not to arrive until the 1960s, with the unleashing of a dramatic demographic, economic and urban expansion. In 1982, the seats of the parliament and of the autonomous governments were fixed here and it became the official capital of Andalusia. In 1992 the city hosted the World's Fair resulting in the improvement of its infrastructures – bridges, freeways, high-speed trains – establishing the foundations for the current Seville, a population of seven hundred thousand inhabitants surrounded by an extensive greater metropolitan area and immersed in modernity, resulting in a city that has known how to reconcile the past with the present, preserving its identity and keeping its traditions alive, something that can be seen in the spectacular and much renowned Spring celebrations during Semana Santa (Holy Week) and the Feria de Abril.

Real Alcázar and Santa Cruz district seen from the Giralda. ▶

The monument district

Seville's historic district, one of the most extensive in Europe, corresponds to the area that was demarcated by the medieval city walls. The most appreciable nucleus is located towards the south, near the river. This is the location of the monuments that were declared World Heritage Sites in 1987: the Cathedral, the Alcázar and the Archivo de Indias.

Cathedral. ▶

The Santa Cruz district

The most seductive and traditional face of Seville is found in the narrow labyrinth of this old and intimate neighborhood, perfumed with the scent of orange blossoms from the streets and jasmine from the interior courtyards. A sinuous network of alleys, tiny plazas, and *adarves* under the shadow of the Giralda and the battlements of the Alcázar that has preserved its medieval character from when it was the Jewish Quarter, and the romantic halo given to it by the adventures of Don Juan Tenorio and the presence of other figures such as Bartolomé Esteban Murillo, the Sevillian master painter. The streetlamp in the plaza de la Virgen de los Reyes, between the Cathedral and the reddish façade of the Archbishop's Palace, marks the beginning of the only somewhat wide street in the neighborhood, calle Mateos Gago, which leads towards the Baroque parish of Santa Cruz, leaving the palaces of calle Abades on one side, and on the other, a

Calle Mesón del Moro (above). ▲
Archbishop's Palace (below).
Plaza de la Virgen de los Reyes (above). ▶▶
Plaza de la Alianza (below).

crooked passageway full of twists and surprises such as: the plaza de la Alianza, across from the Christ made of *azulejos* (painted tiles); calle Santa Teresa and the convent founded by this Saint opposite the traditional Sevillian style house where Murillo once lived, with its central courtyard surrounded by high and low rooms alternatively used in winter and summer months; the plaza de doña Elvira, once the site of open-air comedies; and very close, the hospital de los Venerables, located in the heart of the district. Originally used to house priests and today a cultural foundation, it has a distinguished Baroque collection from the 17th century; contrasting white and red ochre colored facades; a garden courtyard, flanked by hallways; and a church with brilliant frescos by Juan de Valdés Leal and his son Lucas Valdés.

The neighborhood's friendly local color can be especially sensed in the pasaje (passageway) de la calle Judería (Jewish Quarter), the "alley of whispers" that zigzags along from the patio de las Banderas joining the callejón del Agua, which runs along the length of city wall containing the pipes that supply water to the Alcázar, bordered by courtyards spilling over with flowerpots, past the house where Washington Irving, author of the romantic *Tales from the Alhambra,* once lived, and narrow streets full of legends

Murillo's House (above). ▲
Santa Cruz district (below).
Santa Cruz. Callejón (Alleyway) de Dos Hermanas in the Jewish Quarter. ▶

Jardines (Gardens) de Murillo (above). ▲

Plaza de Santa Cruz (below).

Patio de Banderas (at right). ▶

with names such as Vida, Susona or Pimienta. Tiny crevices that lead little by little to the plaza de Santa Cruz, the embodiment of the traditional image of Seville with its flowerbeds and orange trees circling the artistically forged cruz (cross) de la Cerrajería. In the surrounding areas, the small layout of the Santa Cruz district expands around the plaza de Refinadores, presided over by the monument to Don Juan, towards the paseo de Catalina de Ribera and the Jardines de Murillo (Murillo Gardens), continuing on the same scale past Santa María la Blanca, the church that was once a synagogue, and San Bartolomé, both adjacent but less frequented neighborhoods that also made up Seville's Jewish Quarter.

The Cathedral

The Cathedral is one of the most outstanding monuments in Seville and in Spain. Its enormous stone structure, crowned by the tower of the Giralda, was raised between the avenida de la Constitución and the Santa Cruz neighborhood, marking the heart of the city's monument district.

Sevillan courtyards. ▲

Built on a lot measuring 160 by 145 meters, with an expansion of more than twenty thousand square meters, it is considered to be the largest Gothic structure in the world and one of Christianity's first cathedrals. It was declared a World Heritage Site in 1987 together with the Alcázar (royal palace-fortress) and the Archivo de Indias (Indian Archives), which are located in the immediate area. This largest church in Spain occupies what was once the site of the Great Mosque built by the Almohads at the end of the 7th century and adapted to the Catholic faith after the conquest of Seville by Ferdinand III in the 8th century. In 1401, however, the ecclesiastical council decided to demolish the Islamic structure to make way for a new temple in the Christian architectural styles of the era. From the very beginning it was made clear that they wished to surpass all known structures and build, according to legend, "a church so big that all who see it will think we are mad". A little over a century later, in 1517, and with the participation of master stone masons from France, Spain, and Germany, the monumental Gothic construction, its rectangular floor plan divided into five naves with attached chapels, was completed. The building inherited the width of the oratory's proportions from the ancient mosque, as well as the adjacent ablution courtyard and the Giralda, the minaret that gave the call to prayer, converted into a bell tower. The Gothic structure was later finished off with various chapels and adjoining rooms in the Renaissance and Baroque styles, designed by architects like Diego de Riaño or Hernán Ruiz el Joven, prolonging its construction until the beginning of the 20th century when all of the Cathedral's facades were finally finished.

The magnificence of this Hispalese cathedral is evident upon circling the building along the Gradas (Steps), the platforms of stairs and columns that defined the jurisdiction of the Church. This famous space, cited by authors such as Cervantes, was where businessmen, merchants and a swarm of scoundrels gathered during Seville's age of splendor in the 16th and 17th centuries. The main gate, the puerta del Perdón (the gate of Pardon) opens on the north side of this complex, characterized by the horseshoe arch, inscriptions in Arabic, Renaissance sculptures and the immense bronze plated Almohad door that leads to the patio de los Naranjos (courtyard of the Orange Trees), a peaceful area planted with fruit trees around a fountain with a Roman basin where Muslims preformed their ritual washing before entering the

Cathedral and the Giralda. ▶

Cathedral and the patio de los Naranjos. ▲

mosque. Arched galleries flow along the sides of the courtyard and at the foot of the Giralda, in addition to rooms from the Chapterhouse and Columbus Library. One of the most significant Renaissance libraries, it boasts a fabulous collection of manuscripts and books from the Cathedral and from the legacy of Hernando Columbus, the erudite son of the explorer.

The colossal Gothic body of the Cathedral demonstrates a vibrant mixture of cresting, gargoyles, pinnacles, and beautiful doorways. The oldest, from the middle of the 15th century, are on the side of the main façade, called del Nacimiento (Birth) and del Bautismo (Baptism), and adorned with baked clay sculptures by Lorenzo Mercadante de Bretaña. The most popular are those that open up to the plaza de la Virgen de los Reyes and del Triunfo (Triumph) – the gates of los Palos and de Campanillas – from the end of the 15th century which are decorated with terracottas by Miguel Florentín. More recent are the large gates at the foot and transepts of the cruciform, finished between the 19th and 20th centuries.

Inside, the magnitude of the space is moving, with a forest of robust columns and vaults reaching up to 36 meters high in the central nave. A majestic atmosphere bathed in the soft light that filters through stained glass windows depicting sacred figures and motifs. The Main Chapel is located in the crossing, under the sumptuous Gothic altar which, studded with reliefs and figures, is the largest altarpiece in the Christian world. The nearby seats of the choir stalls are Gothic-Mudejar in style and there are spectacular Baroque organs. In one transept, opposite a gigantic mural of San Cristóbal, lies the mausoleum of Christopher Columbus, whose contents are still the subject of controversy. Along the length of the temple are chapels and rooms containing a vast heritage of altarpieces, sculptures, paintings, jewels, precious metals, and other pieces of art that make the Cathedral the richest and most varied of the city's museums. At the head of the temple is the Capilla Real (Royal Chapel), a Renaissance apse presided over by the Virgen de los Reyes – patron saint of Seville – and the pantheon with the remains of San Ferdinand, Alfonso X the Wise, Peter I and other members of Spanish royalty. Next to it, the chapel of San Pedro exhibits an pictorial retable by Zurbarán, adding to the somber collection of masterpieces in the chapels lining up along the sides of the church, at its foot and around the choir, such as: the Virgen de la Antigua, which has the image of the

The Giralda (above). ▸
Puerta del Perdón of the Cathedral (below).
Puerta de la Concepción and patio de los Naranjos. ▸▸

Virgin said to have been found by Ferdinand III upon his conquest of the city; San Antonio, which contains an unusually sized painting by Murillo; or the chapels of the Alabastros (Alabasters), carefully built with this material and housing unique pieces such as the Inmaculada (Blessed Virgin) known as *La Cieguecita* by the sculptor Martínez Montañés.

Special attention should also be given to the rooms on the southern side of the Cathedral: the sacristy de los Cálices (Chalices), where there is a painting of the *Santas (Saints) Justa and Rufina* by Goya, and valuable medieval panels; the Main Sacristy, a marvel of Renaissance architecture where the treasury is located, containing the shrine of the *Custodia*, the processional vessel of the Corpus made of 100 kilograms of silver and a jeweled triptych with the *Tablas Alfonsíes*, among other works of art such as oil paintings by Murillo and Zurbarán; and the Chapterhouse, the surprising elliptical room used for council meetings and covered by a dome with paintings by Murillo. The Cathedral complex is completed by the parish church of the Sagrario, added in the 17th century to a

Cathedral, "Seises" being danced at the High Altar. ▲

Cathedral, cruciform vault. ▶

Cathedral, Naves of the choir and the organ. ▶▶

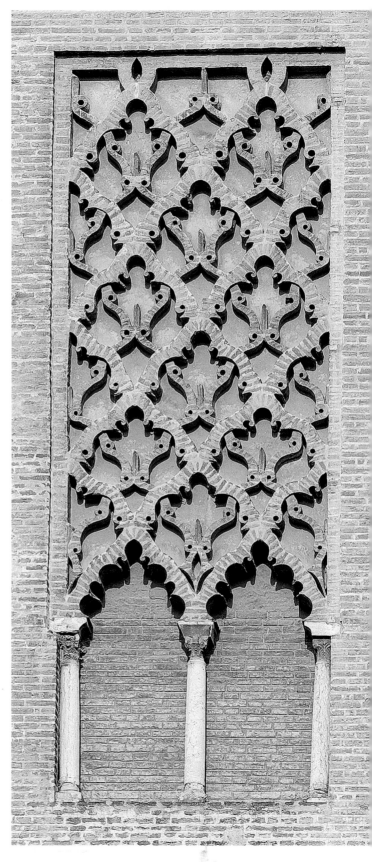

side of the patio de los Naranjos. Its emphatic Baroque vaults shelter a moving altarpiece by the religious artist Pedro Roldán.

The Giralda

Rising up between the patio de los Naranjos and the Cathedral, this tower, converted into the symbol of Seville, is emblematic of the long history and cultural mixing that characterizes the city. Commissioned by the Almohad Caliph Abu Yaqub Yusuf as the minaret for the great mosque, it was completed in 1198 under the direction of the master builders Ahmed Ibn Baso and Alí de Gomara. Situated on a base of ashlars and with a slender shaft made of brickwork and decorated with lengths of cut brick, it is identical to the minaret of the Kutubiyya de Marrakech Mosque and the tower of Hassan de Rabat, in Morocco. Inside, the tower has a ramp rather than stairs, that allowed a horse to reach the top. The Giralda acquired its form, magnitude and definitive name after the Christian conquest, remaining the most harmonious example of the cultural amalgam. In 1568 the architect Hernán Ruiz

The Giraldillo (above). ▲

The Giralda. Brickwork and windows. ▶

el Joven finished it off with a Renaissance bell tower, crowned by a 3.5 meter high bronze statue representing the triumph of faith which serves as a weathervane.

The popular name for this figure – the Giraldillo, the Giralda, after its constant revolving movement – ended up as the name for the entire tower, which reaches 95 meters in height. Aside from being the city's first monument, the Giralda also boasts the best views of Seville, the vantage point that dominates the extensive horizon of the historic city under a landscape of towers and belfries.

Archivo de Indias (Indian Archives)

The most assessed example of Renaissance architecture in Seville sits on a pedestal in front of the Alcázar and the plaza del Triunfo. This solid two-story construction, made up of pure lines, masonry and brick, a square floor plan, and a central courtyard and cloister, was erected between 1583 and 1598 during the reign of Philip II, under the supervision of his favorite architect, Juan de Herrera, the architect of El Escorial. Used as a Merchant's Guild, its construction was motivated by complaints from the Church that the cathedral was being used for merchant meetings. In 1785, Charles III ordered that all

Archivo de Indias. Façade (above). ▲
Archivo de Indias and gardens (below).
Archivo de Indias. ▶

documents relating to the kingdom overseas (the New World) be gathered and stored here, and the building was converted into the Indian Archives. Since then, it has been home to the world's most complete collection of documents relating to the history of America and the Pacific between the 15th and 19th centuries, with 90 million pages of manuscripts and 7,000 maps and drawings. Recently it has incorporated rooms from the nearby Cilla del Cabildo building, an old grain storage building whose coat of arms – the Giralda standing between two jars of Madonna lilies – is above the door.

In front of the Cathedral, the ecclesiastical seat of Seville, is the temporary seat of power, the Real Alcázar. Situated to the south of the historic district, this vast fortress and palace has served as a residence for governors, sultans, caliphs, emperors, and kings, since its seed was commissioned by the Cordoban Emir Abderramán III in the year 913. For the next one thousand years, its trajectory would become a reflection of the vicissitudes of the city itself, while within its walls there remain echoes of memorable figures and events from every era, as well as the architectural imprint of the cultures that

Real Alcázar. City walls (above). ▲

Real Alcázar. Puerta del León. ▶

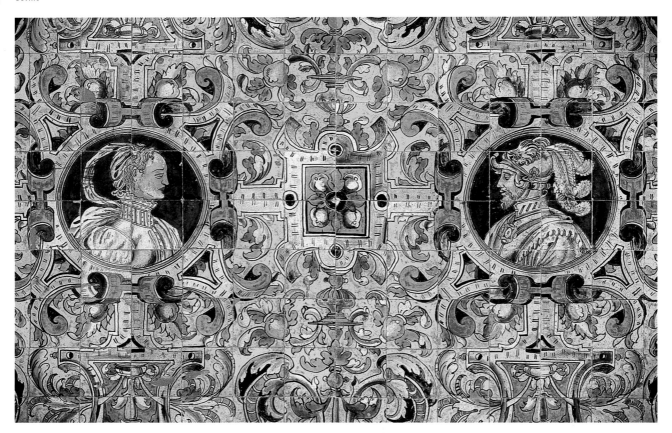

have followed over time, weaving together a fascinating mosaic of history and art. Vastly different from other European royal palaces, the Alcázar better embodies the model of an Eastern citadel, where the palatine nuclei superimpose one another over time following incredibly diverse styles, which, in this case span Islamic and Mudejar art, in addition to Gothic, Renaissance, Baroque, and other 19th and 20th century movements. Its oldest sector, the plaza de Armas (Arms courtyard) of the primitive 10th century alcázar, can be seen in the walls facing the plaza del Triunfo and the patio de Banderas (Flags courtyard), with the beautiful backdrop of the Cathedral. The Alcázar's subtle combinations of spaces and forms begin upon passing through the main gate known as the puerta del León (gate of the Lion). The large 14th century Mudejar room of the sala de la Justicia is juxtaposed by the reflecting pool and the refined fretwork tracings of the patio del Yeso (Plaster courtyard), a direct vestige from the Almohads who used walls, houses and gardens in the 12th and 13th centuries to make the Alcázar an enviable oasis.

Real Alcázar. Detail of azulejos to Renaissance (above). ▲
Bedroom window, Patio de las Doncellas (below).
Real Alcázar. Arco de los Pavones (Arch of the Peacocks). ▶

The arcaded colonnade of the cuarto del Almirante (Admiral's room) runs along a length of the outer wall. This was the location of the Casa de la Contratación (Contract House), the organism that regulated the Sevillian monopoly on traffic between Castile and the Indies. The painting of the Virgen de los Mareantes on its chapel's altarpiece, painted by Alejo Fernández in 1536, offers valuable documentation of some of the protagonists of the American companies, such as Columbus, Charles V and Magallanes. The patio de la Montería (Hunting courtyard) flaunts the large interior façade of the Alcázar, articulated by the majestic brick, plasterwork, and Arabic inscriptions on the palace of King Don Pedro, a masterpiece of the Mudejar style – the stylistic Christian-Muslim hybrid – begun in 1364, and collaborated on by artisans from Toledo, Granada, and Seville. On the lower level, passageways and rooms are distributed around two courtyards, that of las Muñecas (the Dolls), which was the secluded and intimate axis of the royal family's private quarters, while that of las Doncellas (the Maidens), was the center of courtesan life, flanked by the dynamism of its groups of lobed arches. The exquisite skill of the Mudejar artisans can be observed along the length of the rooms with their ceramic surfaces, tiled baseboards and coffered ceilings all revolving around the

Real Alcázar. Palace of King don Pedro (above left). ▲
Real Alcázar. Patio de las Doncellas (above right).
Real Alcázar. Salón de Embajadores. ▶

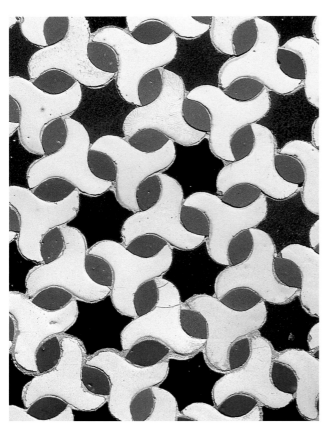

spectacular salón de Embajadores (Ambassador's Room), the throne room and reception hall based in the walls and arches of the 11th century pavilion once used by the kings of Sevillian taifas, and sheltered by a marvelous wooden dome assembled by the carpenter Diego Roiz in 1427.

The royal rooms continue on the upper floor of the palace, decorated following a similar pattern with meticulous polychrome plasterwork and tiling. The patio del Crucero (Crossing courtyard), the subterranean garden of Almohad origin which contained Mrs. María de Padilla's bathing pool, serves as a transit point to the Gothic palace. Its somber exteriors and fortified appearance were constructed in the 13th century by Alfonso X and renovated in the 16th and 18th centuries. Its rooms were the setting for the intellectual pursuits of the Wise King (Alfonso X), author of the Cantigas de Santa María (medieval poems) and other varied writings, and for the wedding of the Emperor Charles V and Isabel of Portugal. In addition to the Italian style *azulejos* and the altarpiece of the Virgen de la Antigua in the chapel, its rooms contain a masterly collection of Flemish tapestries that nar-

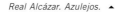

Real Alcázar. Azulejos. ▲

Real Alcázar. Mrs. María de Padilla's Baths. ▶

Real Alcázar. Cenador del León. ▲

Real Alcázar. Jardín de los Poetas. ▶

rate the Emperor's conquest of Tunisia in 1535. Next to the palace lies the sensual seven hectare extension that makes up the Alcázar gardens, one of most essential examples of Spanish gardening. The peaceful Spanish-Muslim courtyards and patios surrounding the buildings give way to the mannerist approach taken in the garden of the Estanque (Pond) and the galería de Grutescos, an elevated path running along a stretch of the Arab wall masked by fountains and rustic ornamental motifs. This path continues through the vegetation and flowers from the various different gardens: las Damas (the Ladies); la Danza (the Dance), which has geometric flowerbeds and spurts of water from the ground; el Cenador (the Bower), known for its delicate Moorish-Classical Charles I pavilion; el León (the Lion), with its Baroque arbor; and el Laberinto (Labyrinth) made out of myrtle hedges; until coming to the meadows of the jardín Inglés (English garden), and the Sevillian style ponds, arbors, and flowerbeds of the jardines Nuevos (New gardens). The route around the Alcázar comes to an end at the saddle and carriage area, known as the Apeadero, next to the patio de Banderas.

Real Alcázar. Fuente de Mercurio (Fountain of Mercury). ▲

Real Alcázar. Estanque de Mercurio and the galería de los Grutescos. ▶

The City Center and the neigh-borhoods

Just a few steps away from the Cathedral and the Santa Cruz district is the City Center, the area within the historic district where public and commercial activity take place, centered around notable buildings such as City Hall or the Ayuntamiento and popular streets like calle Sierpes. The surrounding areas are residential, interspersed with monuments like the Casa de Pilatos and the Museum of Fine Arts, while the more traditional and modest neighborhoods are spread out towards the north along the calles Feria and San Luis, towards the Alameda de Hércules and the walls of the Macarena.

"El Jueves" street market on the calle Feria. ▶

City Hall and calle Sierpes

The location of the Casa Consistorial is like the balance point between the two plazas that define the center of Seville. On one side is the plaza de San Francisco, a public forum once used for markets, autos-da-fé, and bull events, and today used for the assembly of the boxes and altars for the Semana Santa and Corpus processions. On the other side is the plaza Nueva, the largest square in the Center, presided over by an equestrian statue of San Fernando, and laid out in the 19th century on the site of a demolished Franciscan convent. The duality of the City Hall is evidenced by its very design, located between these two plazas whose different characters are reflected the building's two facades. The façade facing plaza de San Francisco was begun in 1527 by the mason Diego de Riaño, in order to give the consistory a dignified style worthy of the booming municipality's rank. He constructed a splendid plateresque façade with reliefs featuring the city's mythical founders – Hercules and Caesar – as well as the symbol of Seville: the hieroglyph NO8DO, that should be read "NO madeja DO", "no me ha dejado" ("you didn't leave me"), the motto that King Alfonso X bestowed upon the city for its

Plaza de San Francisco (above). ▲
Plaza Nueva. Monument to San Fernando (below).
City Hall. Façade facing the plaza de San Francisco. ▶

loyalty to him during the dynastic conflicts with his son. The entrance, *apeadero* (place to mount or dismount a horse) and lower Chapterhouse correspond to the canons of the early Renaissance, while the staircase, upper rooms and upper Chapterhouse denote a more evolved style.

In contrast, the body of the *Ayuntamiento* or City Hall, facing the Plaza Nueva, reflects a more austere Neoclassical style from the 19th century. The municipal rooms boast an admirable pictorial collection that includes paintings such as the *Imposition de la casulla a San Ildefonso,* by Velázquez, or the *Inmaculada Concepción* by Zurbarán. Just a few steps away from City Hall is calle Sierpes, the oldest and most traditional artery of Seville. Pedestrian by definition, narrow, irregular, varied and boisterous, its atmosphere takes on an even more Sevillian tone in the hottest months when the streets are shaded by canvases. In the neighboring areas going towards La Campana and plaza del Duque, other essential focal points in the City Center, there are several small areas worth noting. These include the Baroque jewel of the chapel of San José and the pleasant plaza del Salvador, whose many bars stand opposite the monumental Baroque church of the Divino Salvador, whose deep Sevillian roots were laid on top of a Roman temple, a

City Hall and the symbol of Seville (above). ▼
Parish of the Divino Salvador (below).
Calle Sierpes, bar Laredo (above). ▶
Calle Sierpes, pastry shop La Campana (below).

Calle Sagasta near calle Sierpes. ▲

Visigoth basilica, and a mosque of which the ablution court-yard still survives.

Casa de Pilatos (House of Pilate)

In the entrails of the historic district, across from a brief plaza made uneven by the San Esteban parish, lies the Casa de Pilatos. The most important of Seville's grand houses, it belongs to the ducal House of Medinaceli. Its original name comes from the first station – Jesus before Pilate – from a Stations of the Cross that was begun at the palace gates, or according to legend from the fact that it is a copy of the palaces of the Roman praetorian governors of Jerusalem. This tradition was inspired by the true story of its instigator, Don Fadrique Enríquez de Ribera, an archetypical patron of the Renaissance Movement who undertook its construction upon his return from a long journey through Europe and a pilgrim-age to the Holy Land in 1519. From his wanderings, Don Fadrique brought with him an appreciation for Classical art that he introduced in a novel way to the Gothic and Mudejar styles that at that time dominated Sevillian architecture, cre-ating a unique building characterized by the synthesis of materials and styles.

Casa de Pilatos. Gardens. ▲

Casa de Pilatos. Main courtyard. ▶

One example is the Renaissance marble door that marks the palace entrance and provides access to the *apeadero,* connected to the stables. This piece was commissioned in a workshop in Genoa in 1529, along with many other elements from the palace. This is followed by the sumptuous main courtyard which has a double gallery of arches and artwork that includes a Carrera marble fountain, Greek and Roman sculptures, Renaissance busts of emperors, Gothic plasterwork and Mudejar tiled baseboards with metallic reflections.

This level of maximum refinement continues on the lower floor along the length of rooms covered in stuccoes, coffering and elaborate woodwork; in the chapel with its ribbed vault; and in the corridors, pavilions, and loggias of the Grande (Large) and Chico (Small) gardens, which are littered with statues, reliefs, and archeological artifacts. A majestic staircase sheathed in ceramics and sheltered by a wooden dome leads to the upper floor, where the dense artistic display continues. Frescos depicting figures from Antiquity and allegories of the four seasons decorate the walls of the hallways and rooms, and in various places, including the dining room, there are tapestries and oil paintings by artists like Pantoja de la Cruz, Carreño and Lucas Jordán. There is also a room with ceilings depicting mythological representations painted in 1603 by Francisco Pacheco, the mentor and father-in-law of the Sevillian painter Diego Velázquez.

Museum of Fine Arts (Museo de Bellas Artes)

A tranquil plaza with a statue of Murillo, large rubber trees and a magnolia lead up to the museum, a site worthy of the second most important museum in Spain which occupies the old convent of the Merced Calzada, founded in the 8th century, restored at the beginning of the 17th century and reformed to house the museum in the 19th century. This museum brings together exceptional collections of painting and sculpture from the Middle Ages to the 20th century, the most complete series from the Sevillian Baroque School, as well as pottery, furniture, architecture and the decorative arts.

The physiognomy of the building follows the general lines of its earlier Medieval restoration undertaken in 1602 by the architect Juan de Oviedo, who gave form to a mannerist esthetic organized around various courtyards, with a monumental staircase and a voluminous church. The foyer, studded with brightly colored figurative painted tiles, leads

Casa de Pilatos. Fuente (fountain) de Jano in the main courtyard (above). ▼
Casa de Pilatos. Detail of Mudéjar plasterwork (below).
Casa de Pilatos. Main courtyard. ▶

to the patio (courtyard) del Aljibe, also decorated with panels and baseboards made of Sevillian *azulejos,* the small garden of the patio de las Conchas and the patio de los Boyes, a model example of geometry and the equilibrium of mannerism.

These courtyards serve as entrances to the first rooms containing art from the end of the Middle Ages with gilded panels in styles falling between Gothic, Flemish and the beginning of the Renaissance Movement, together with notable sculptures such as the terracotta *Virgen con el Niño* by Lorenzo Mercadante de Bretaña. Organized chronologically, they are followed by a selection of art from the 16th century that reflects the formation of the local Pictorial School and other pieces from artists of varying backgrounds, including: the *Stations of the Cross* by Lucas Cranach; the striking statue of *San Jerónimo* made of polychrome baked clay, sculpted in 1525 by the peer and rival of Miguel Ángel Pietro Torrigiano; and the serene *portrait of Jorge Manuel Theotocopoulos,* painted by his father, El Greco, in 1600.

The dawn of Sevillian art between the 16th and 17th centuries is an indication of the city's zenith on all levels, and can be contemplated in various religious carvings and oil paintings by artists such as Juan de las Roelas or

Monument to Murillo and the Museum of Fine Arts (above). ▲
Museum of Fine Arts. Church room (below).
Museum of Fine Arts. Panels of Baroque azulejos. ▶

Francisco Pacheco, whose workshop was the starting place for the young Velázquez. The prosperity of this local school is captured in the extraordinary church, an atmosphere of generous proportions and vaulted ceilings decorated with frescos in harmony with the large formats of Zurbarán, Murillo, and other masters.

Francisco de Zurbarán, who came to Seville from the province of Extremadura, depicted the figures of saintly monks as well as his 1631 masterpiece the *Apoteosis de Santo Tomás de Aquino.* The mastery of Murillo can be admired in the head of the church, where there is a *colossal Virgin,* images of the *Santas Justa and Rufina, Santo Tomás de Villanueva, Our Lady of Sorrows,* and other displays of his fluent brush strokes and soft colors, a style that is condensed, as in a jar of essences, in the small *Virgin de la servilleta,* radiating the magic of its intimate expressiveness and colors safeguarded in the shadow of a niche.

The large cloister and imperial staircase with imaginative plasterwork lead the way to the upper floor, which is dominated by a 17th century Baroque revival by Sevillian painters as well as other Spaniards, Flemish and Italians. Once again, Zurbarán displays his mastery of lines and color – seen in the series of la Cartuja – , and José de Ribera exhibits the precise naturalism of vehement chiaroscuros, while the energetic drama of the Sevillian Juan de Valdés Leal, is emphasized in compositions such as his depictions of San Jerónimo. Students of Murillo and Hispalese painting from the 18th century are the focus of the contiguous spaces in this museum, whose founding was nurtured by the abundance of artistic heritage coming from the dozens of convents and religious foundations that were dismantled in the first half of the 19th century as a result of the War of Independence and the laws of the liberal governments.

Two small Goya paintings and the galleries containing portraits and historical paintings from the Romantic period make up the final wing of the museum, which also includes some landscapes and traditional paintings from the last Sevillian school, such as the popular oil painting called *Las Cigarreras* by Gonzalo Bilbao.

Other monuments in the historic district

Seville is a city for memories, and an infinite city, one of "those exquisite things – said a traveler in days gone by – that the more you see them, the more they bring you joy". Next to the city's most unique and well-known monuments, there is a densely woven network of places so interesting

Roque Balduque. Virgen con el niño *(above).* ▲
Murillo. Santas Justa y Rufina *(below).*
Zurbarán. San Hugo in the refectory *(above).* ▶
Gonzalo Bilbao. Las Cigarreras *(below).*

that they would be the highlights of many other cities. The church of the Magdalena stands out in the traditional neighborhoods located in the immediate area that lies towards the river and the Museum of Fine Arts. It forms part of the Dominican convent of San Pablo, which in 1480, was the site of the first court of the Spanish Inquisition. Rebuilt at the end of the 17th century, the church gives an idea of the abuntant weath adquired by Sevillian religious buildings in Baroque times. The exterior lure of a dome decorated with figures of giants and painted tile, corresponds to the splendid interior embellished with frescos, plasterwork, sculptures, a high altarpiece, paintings by Zurbarán and first class religious imagery. In the nearby calle Cuna, the Palace of Lebrija holds another demonstration of artistic content on a civil architecture level. Its surfaces are a recount of mosaics and Roman floors taken from Itálica, while its rooms, with different themes, bring together infinite collections of archeological artifacts.

Deeper into the residential areas of the historic district lies the Mudejar parish of San Lorenzo and the basilica of Nuestro Padre Jesús del Gran Poder, the most solemn of the Semana Santa (Holy Week) processions, attributed to Juan de Mesa. Further along, the streets keep up with the

Calle Feria. "El Jueves" street market (above). ▲
Convent of San Clemente (below).
Church of San Lorenzo. ▶

presence of palaces and large convents such as Santa Ana, Santa Clara and San Clemente. This vast urban circuit of the old city is divided by la Alameda de Hércules. This avenue defines the more modest neighborhoods that dominate the area to the east and the north, where each parish is a microcosm surrounding its Mudejar church: Santa Catalina and San Marcos; the neighborhood of the Feria (Spring Festival) and its churches of San Juan de la Palma and Omnium Sanctorum; the calle San Luis with Santa Marina, a route that passes by mansions like the palace of the Dueñas; convents like the monastery of Santa Paula, a model example of Sevillian cloisters; and unique monuments such as the 18th century church of San Luis, the most dynamic Baroque composition in the city, with Solomonic spiraled columns that rise up towards the fantasy of light and color in the airy dome.

The Macarena

Located at the northern vertex of the historic district, the neighborhood known as the Macarena has a distinct and traditional personality, its most characteristic features being its Arab walls and basilica. The compact hamlet of

Church of San Luis. Dome (above). ▲
Convent of Santa Paula (below).
Church of San Luis. ▶

the Macarena is defined by the most complete stretch of this wall in existence, which has defenses including a moat, walls, towers, and doors built by the Almoravids and Almohads in the 9th century to defend Seville. The arco (arch) de la Macarena stands out in one of its extremes, the ancient entrance refurbished in the Baroque style in the 19th century, and next to it lies the basilica, built in 1949 as a sanctuary for the Virgen de la Esperanza (Hope) – or Esperanza Macarena – the most fervently revered and loved Semana Santa procession.

Across from the arch is the Renaissance façade of the Andalusian Parliament building, once the old hospital de la Sangre or de las Cinco Llagas, built in the middle of the 16th century. Its church, today an assembly room, was designed by Hernán Ruiz el Joven, the architect who designed the Giralda's belfry and it is considered one of the most daring examples of masonry art.

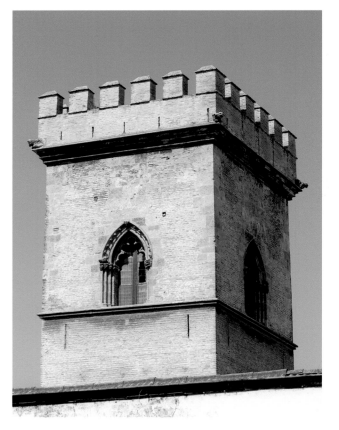

Parliament of Andalusia (above left). ▲
Top of the arco de la Macarena (above right).
Torre Don Fadrique (below). ▶
Nuestra Señora de la Esperanza Macarena. ▶▶

The River and the Park

The Guadalquivir River is the nerve of Seville and the city's most open and luminous façade. Bordered by tree-lined promenades and famous monuments including the torre del Oro (Golden Tower) and the plaza de toros de la Maestranza (Maestranza Bullring), it was once the reason for this city's existence; a city that depended on its river port where the galleons loaded with gold and silver from the Indies would land. More recently, the river has channeled the city's expansion towards the south, along the leafy mass of vegetation of the parque de María Luisa (María Luisa Park) and the urban areas laid out for the celebration of the 1929 Latin American Expo, an event which left behind a legacy of picturesque pavilions and grandiose spaces such as the plaza de España.

Fisherman on the Guadalquivir River. ▶

Torre del Oro and the hospital de la Caridad

This Sevillian symbol is reflected in the river, called the Betis by the Romans, and the "great river", *ued el-kebir,* by the Arabs. The polygonal tower was built by the Almohads around 1220 to defend the access to the port. This was a mission that it must have carried out to perfection during the assault on Seville by Ferdinand III in 1248, who was unable to force the city to surrender until his fleet, under the command of Ramón Bonifaz, cut the chain running between the tower and the opposite riverbank which had prevented the passage of the Christians and made it possible to bring supplies to the city's defenders on the Guadalquivir. This bastion marks the final extreme of the walls that connected the port to the Alcázar. The next link in this chain was the Torre de la Plata (Silver Tower), located between the buildings of the old Casa de la Moneda (Mint), where cargos of silver and gold were brought from America.

The name of the Torre del Oro is still an enigma. It has been attributed to the golden tone that the tower takes on at dusk, as well as to its former purpose of guarding the king's treasures and the precious metals unloaded from the galleons. Today its rooms watch over very different

Paseo de Colón. ▲

Torre del Oro. ▶

contents. There is a small museum about Seville's naval history and river navigation, whose collection includes items such as the designs for the *Betis,* Spain's first steamship, built in the Triana shipyards and launched in Seville in 1817.

The warehouses of the Medieval dockyards line up in the area around the Torres del Oro and de la Plata, the port's arsenal upon which the hospital de la Caridad (Charity Hospital) was raised in the 17th century. A masterpiece of Sevillian Baroque, its building was promoted by the aristocratic merchant Miguel de Mañara, who according to legend, was the inspiration for the dramatic figure of Don Juan. The hospital complex consists of two courtyards with galleries and Italian marble fountains around which the rooms are centered, and a church with ceramic panels painted on the façade. The writing on the church's threshold reads "here lie the bones... of the worst man that the world has ever known"..., the epitaph of Mañara's tomb which culminates the discussion about the fleetingness of life that he himself dictated to the best artists of the time. In fact, inside, there are disturbing canvases of the *Jeroglíficos de las Postrimerías,* allusive to vanity and death, painted by Juan de Valdés Leal in 1672, and various oil paintings from

Atarazanas (above). ▲
Dockyards (below).
Church of Hospital de la Caridad. ▶

Murillo's later years, the most outstanding being those of *Santa Isabel de Hungría* and *San Juan de Dios,* in addition to the Main Altar, adorned with the solemn scene of the *Entierro de Cristo* sculpted by Pedro Roldán.

Plaza de toros de la Maestranza (Maestranza Bullring)

An authentic "cathedral" of bullfighting and a keystone in the history of tauromachy (bullfighting), the Maestranza was one of the first circular bullrings and one of the first made with hewn stone, begun in 1761 and finished over a century later. The Sevillian bullring is also one of the most beautiful, for the brightness of its whitewashed walls, its Baroque entrance with the puerta del Príncipe (gate of the Prince) – only opened for those who triumph –, the carved stone box seating that presides over the ring, and the harmonious relationship between the floor of the bullring – with its characteristic ocher-yellow color – and the stands which are crowned with a ring of arches over marble columns. The name of the plaza comes from its holding institution, the Real Maestranza de Caballería (the Royal Arsenal Cavalry), a noble corporation established in the 17th century to promote the military training of the nobility through equestrianism.

During the afternoon bullfights, the atmosphere of the Maestranza is unmistakable for its colors and liveliness, for the relaxed mood of the spectators (which usually include a number of famous faces), for the ladies adorned in Mantillas (traditional lace headdresses) in the stands next to the Prince's box, and for the impressive silences through which the fans show their respect when the matadors execute a fine series of passes. This atmosphere is evoked just by entering the arena, wandering through the stands, the pens, the stables, the small chapel where bullfighters pray before the opening procession, and the interesting Museo Taurino (Bullfighting Museum). This collection includes a varied repertoire of pieces relating to the bullring and the art of bullfighting, from the wooden scapegoats that were used in chivalrous moves, to sculptures, paintings, bullfighting costumes, and memorabilia from famous bullfighters, as well as a cape signed by Picasso. The bullring, axis of the traditional Arenal district, looks out over the river by way of the paseo de Colón, accompanied by the monuments to the matador Curro Romero and the mythical figure of Carmen, whose final act took place at its entrance.

Plaza de toros de la Maestranza. Detail (above). ▲
Statue of the famed bullfighter Curro Romero (below).
Plaza de toros de la Maestranza. Puerta del Príncipe. ▶

Parque de María Luisa (María Luisa Park)

A leafy expanse of vegetation carpets the area located past the Torre del Oro and the walls of the Alcázar. This domain, outside the city walls, initially consists of a small island garden known as the jardines (gardens) de Christina located very close to the river and to a few notable buildings. One of these is the luxurious Alfonso XIII hotel, with the typical combination of brick, *azulejos* and marble from the Regionalist style that proliferated in Seville around the Latin American Expo in 1929. Another is the 18th century Fábrica de Tabacos (Tobacco Factory), today the University. This enormous block, measuring 185 by 147 meters, was where the thousands of women who inspired the fictitious character of Carmen La Cigarrera, the romantic heroine of freedom and fatal passion, worked. And finally, there is the palace of San Telmo, a Baroque building from the 17th and 18th centuries with an ostentatious white stone door, originally used as a nautical school for pilots in the Race to the Indies, and later home to the tiny court of the Dukes of Montpensier. For the last several years it has been the seat of the Presidency of the Government of Andalusia. Leafy Seville begins to grow behind this palace, created by the

Antigua Real Fábrica de Tabacos, today the University, detail (above). ▼
Antigua Real Fábrica de Tabacos. Main entrance (below).
Antigua Real Fábrica de Tabacos. Courtyard of the University (above). ▶
Hotel Alfonso XIII (below).

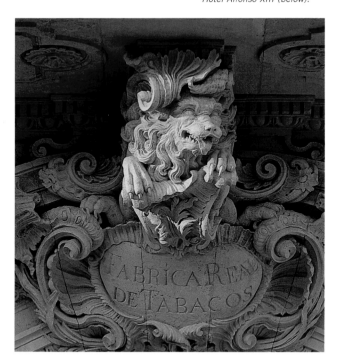

donation of the gardens of San Telmo to the city by the Infanta María Luisa de Borbón, who the park is named after in 1893. Revamped at the beginning of the 20th century by Nicolas Forestier, a park conservationist from Paris, it was given a unique Sevillian character that forged an "alliance between the European promenade, the tranquility of Eastern courtyards and the romantic daydream of the landscape garden". The Latin American Expo of 1929 sparked the addition of monuments, pavilions and other architectural and ornamental elements that turned the Park into an attractive sphere of radiant variety. With an area of 38 hectares and a large botanical diversity including over 3,500 trees and almost 1,000 palm trees, the length of the park is adorned with outstanding brick and painted tile arbors dedicated to artists and writers, as well as ceramic fountains, the Moorish arbor known as Costurero de la Reína, and melancholy corners like the circular glorieta de Bécquer, which has a bust of the Sevillian poet and the likeness of the three stages of love – hoped for, fully conceived, and lost – under a large taxodio or bald cypress tree planted in 1850. Not to mention the view from the park's central axis that runs along the estanque de los Lotos (Lotus pond) and the isleta de los Patos (Duck island), with its exotic oriental temple, to the

Parque de María Luisa. Glorieta de Bécquer (above). ▾
Parque de María Luisa, avenue of Hernán Cortés (below).
Plaza de España, pages 79-81. ▸▸

jets of water in the jardín de los Leones (garden of the Lions) and the cascada del Monte Gurugú, (Mount Gurugú waterfall), a picturesque inclined rock garden.

Plaza de España

During the first third of the 20th century, Seville experienced the feverish effervescence of the preparations for the momentous contest in which great hopes for progress, modernization and international recognition were instilled. This event was the spark behind the city's large southern expansion on the park's axis. After not a few setbacks, in 1929 the Latin American Expo was finally opened, an ephemeral occasion but one that had long term effects on the city's urban landscape. Several of the most representative monuments in Seville sprang from its tangible legacy, such as the plaza de España, the landmark located in the middle of the parque María Luisa.

The plaza de España is made up of a semicircle of astonishing magnitude, marked by two 80 meter high towers. A small river runs between these two pointed masts, staggered by bridges, and there is a walkway following a series of panels made of painted *azulejos,* as well as a gallery of arches over columns. Finished in 1928 and used as the host country pavilion in the 1929 Expo, the plaza was designed by Aníbal González, the architect most inspired by Sevillian regionalism. The plaza is covered in reddish brick, cut and sized with numerous pieces of painted and glazed polychrome ceramic, creating a symphony of tones and shimmers that come to life in the light of dusk.

Museums in the plaza de América

The plaza de América is a fundamental space both for the distribution of its buildings and for their content. Centered around a pond and a small plaza filled with the flutter of doves below a tuft of palm trees, one of its sides is adorned with the graceful rhythm of the arcades and filigree of the Pabellón Mudejar (Mudejar Pavilion). This Moorish style construction carried out by Aníbal González in 1914, houses the Museum of Arts and Local Customs, which contains select collections of pottery, jewels and precious metal work, embroideries and clothing, as well as musical instruments and numerous artifacts having to do with agriculture, popular religion, celebrations, and traditional trades.

The Archeological Museum occupies the most somber of the pavilions, located on the opposite side of the square. The

Plaza de España. Detail of the azulejos (above). ▾
Plaza de España. Detail of the semicircle (below).
Plaza de España. Central fountain. ▸
Patios of the Casino de la Exposición, pages 84-85. ▸▸

intense confluence of people and civilizations in Western Andalusia since Prehistoric times has been captured in the detailed showcase of this museum, considered to be the region's most distinguished in this sphere. The first sections bring together stone tools, pottery and household goods from the peninsula's dolmens, and of note are the Phoenician and Tartessian artifacts, idolillos, candelabras, and especially the collection of gold pieces from the treasury of Carambolo, testament to the opulence of the Kingdom of Tartessos, which, located in what are today the provinces of Seville and Huelva, provided precious metals to all of the Mediterranean in the 7th and 8th centuries BC. This is immediately followed by a collection of Iberian reliefs and Roman artifacts which form the principal nucleus of the museum's collection.

The Roman artifacts include everyday items such as glassware, coins, mosaics, bronzes, altar stones and sepulchers and create a context for the impressive collection of sculptures, the majority of which are from Itálica, with figures of gods and magnificent depictions of Venus, Mercury, Alexander the Great, Trajan and Hadrian among others.

Royal Pavilion. ▲

Museum of Arts and Local Customs. ▶

Triana and the Cartuja

The course of the Guadalquivir River divides the Sevillian capital leaving the extensive historic district on one bank and the modest district of Triana on the other. A traditional neighborhood, Triana is known for being lively and happy, and over time it has been surrounded by large modern urban areas laid out along the river. Among these, the most striking is, without a doubt, the large area known as the Cartuja, which served as the site of the 1992 World's Fair. The historic monastery that lent its name to this district is surrounded by spectacularly modern and contemporary structures, providing a sharp contrast to the traditional image of Seville.

Puente de Triana (Triana Bridge over the Guadalquivir River). ▸

Triana

Located on the right bank of the Guadalquivir River, across from Seville – it is only natural to differentiate between the banks of Seville and Triana, with their distinctly different personalities – stretch the streets of this ancient district of sailors, potters, gypsies, artisans and wayfarers of all classes. Famed for being lively and happy, this area has always been a hotbed of Flamenco artists and bullfighters. With a propensity for speculation and legend, its name is said to have come from the Emperor Trajan, while the development of Triana is attributed to Muslim times, and above all the age when the Sevillian port canalized relations with America.

The puente (bridge) "of iron" or de Isabel II, was the first fixed bridge built over Sevillian waters. Inaugurated in 1852, it is the umbilical cord that connects the capital to this more modest district, letting out next to the market erected on the foundations of the castle of San Jorge, the fortress of the Inquisition of which only the outline of the courtyard and the lower rooms remain like a sinister warning. The neighborhood's open and lineal weave runs parallel to the Guadalquivir, terraced as of the wonderful river-

Puente de Triana (above). ▲
Puente de Triana, detail (below).
Terraces in the calle Betis. ▶

front façade of the calle Betis, without a doubt one of the most beautiful in the city with its embankments and brightly painted houses and excellent views of the panorama of Seville including the plaza de toros, the Torre del Oro, the Cathedral and the Giralda. The district's interior artery is the calle Pureza – which is nothing like its name (purity) – dotted with the chapel of the Virgen de la Esperanza, mistress of the devotion of the people of Triana, and the parish of Santa Ana, an incipient Gothic church that serves as the neighborhood's cathedral.

The flavor of Triana permeates the calles San Jacinto, Alfarería, and Castilla, brimming with pottery workshops selling the famed ceramics, taverns where Flamenco can still be heard, shared courtyards filled with flowerpots and plants, and the chapels that are the heart and soul of this modest area. They include Nuestra Señora de la O, the Patrocinio, the sanctuary of the Cristo de la Expiración, known as "el Cachorro" to the gypsies – once again legends are everywhere – whose agony was captured by the religious artist Ruiz Gijón who carved this moving crucifix.

Detail of azulejos in the Triana district (above). ▲
Barrio de Triana. Display of ceramics from Triana (abajo).
Triana district. Ceramics shop. ▶

Puente de Triana and monument complex of the Cartuja. ▲

The Cartuja

Upriver from Triana, also on the right-hand bank of the
Guadalquivir, is the area known as the Cartuja, site of the
1992 World's Fair. In the middle of this mixed landscape of
old pavilions, office buildings and recreational activities is
the monument complex of the Cartuja de Santa María de la
Cuevas, which stood alone until the 1980s, surrounded by
fields of crops. This lot, once home to one of the richest
monasteries in Seville, is defined by a high wall that serves
as a parapet against floods. Founded in approximately
1399, the monastery was an incumbent to the patronage of
the Ribera, owners of the Casa de Pilatos, and the favor of
prominent figures such as Christopher Columbus. Its des-
tiny however, changed in the 19th century when it was converted into a ceramics factory, and again in the 20th century upon its transformation into the Royal Pavilion of the
World's Fair, and then into the seat of the Andalusian
Contemporary Art Center. The Cartuja includes a varying
series of buildings and atmospheres ranging from the
Capilla Pública (Public Chapel) at the entrance, to the spa-
cious bowered gardens, and the central nucleus made up of
the nave of the 15th century church and the chapel of

Monastery of the Cartuja (above). ▲
Puente del V Centenario (below).
Ovens from the old ceramics factory of the Cartuja. ▶

Santa Ana (where the remains of Columbus were temporarily kept). Not to mention the small Mudejar cloister with its annexes to the refectory, the room containing portentous Renaissance sepulchers made in Genoa in 1530, and the cloisters that were rebuilt using a current interpretation of the original cylindrical kilns used in the ceramics factory.

The structures built for the World's Fair – the Auditorium; the Navigation, Future, Spanish and Andalusian pavilions... – and newer buildings like the Olympic Stadium, cover the area of the Cartuja all the way to the banks of the river, cut by the modern bridges of the Barqueta and Alamillo, the most striking of all, by Santiago Calatrava. With a 138 meter tall pylon – the city's first structure to rise higher than the Giralda – and hanging cables that hold the 200 meter long platform, it has quickly become the symbol of contemporary Seville.

Puente de la Barqueta. ▲
Puente del Alamillo. ▶

The Province

Seville is surrounded by an infinity of interesting places that warrant a visit. Nearby are the ruins of the exceptional Roman city of Itálica, and immediately following, the hills of the Aljarafe dotted with pueblos blancos or white towns, and the lower course of the Guadalquivir River in the middle of an immense horizon of marshlands. Further inland and stretching out into the countryside, are the cities of Carmona, Écija, Osuna and other large towns that display an extraordinary artistic heritage of the purest Andalusian flavor, while the northern extreme boasts the province's most mountainous territory, in the form of the Sierra Norte of Seville.

Itálica. Casa del Planetario (Planetarium House). ▸

Itálica. Roman road. ▲
Itálica. Ruins of the amphitheater. ▶

Itálica, the Aljarafe and the Marismas

Very close to Seville and next to the town of Santiponce, lies one of the most important Roman sites on the Peninsula: Itálica, the city founded in the year 206 BC by Scipio Africanus. An aristocratic city from the beginning, it was the birthplace of the great Roman emperors Trajan and Hadrian, who greatly enriched the city with splendid projects. In fact, the majority of the excavated area corresponds to the enlargement of the city carried out by Hadrian at the beginning of the 2nd century AD. Some of the most outstanding sights in Itálica are the amphitheater, the third largest in the Roman world with an estimated capacity of 25,000 spectators, and the checkerboard of tiled streets and mansions with luxurious mosaics, such as those found in the casas de los Pájaros (House of the Birds) and del Planetario (of the Planetarium), next to the remains of baths and temples. The town of Santiponce boasts the ruins of the Roman theater and the monastery of San Isidoro del Campo, a jewel of Gothic-Mudejar art founded in 1301 by Guzmán el Bueno. The sepulcher of this legendary figure lies here, as do valuable frescos from the 15th century and an altarpiece with sculptures by Martínez Montañés.

The Aljarafe plateau juts out above Itálica to the west of Seville. Made up of a pleasant hamlet of towns and haciendas (estates) nestled between olive groves and vineyards, today it is considered part of the city's metropolitan area. Its surrounding areas abound with evocative places such as: the Prehistoric dolmens of Valencina de la Concepción; the ancient Almohad mosque of Cuatrovitas in Bollullos; the Fransciscan convent of Loreto located close to Espartinas; the monumental church and the wineries of Umbrete, the palace that was the home of the celebrated count-duke; and the Mudejar churches and haciendas like that of Benazuza, found in Sanlúcar la Mayor. To the south of Aljarafe lie the Marismas, the wetlands of the Guadalquivir, an endless landscape of rice fields, channels and marshes, teeming with birds and located at the entrance to the Doñana National Park.

Olivares. Plaza and the Collegiate Church. ▲
Boat on the Guadalquivir in Coria del Río. ▶

The Campiña (countryside), from Carmona and Écija to Osuna

The undulating countryside known as the campiña, the most fertile land in Andalusia, unfolds to the east of Seville along the Guadalquivir Valley, studded with the impressive pueblos blancos (white towns), which are of monumental importance. Carmona, located at the edge of the Alcores hills, brings together one of the most historically rich groupings in Southern Spain.

On the edge of the city is the Roman Necropolis (1st century BC - 4th century AD), a funerary complex with hundreds of tombs dug out of the rocks. Farther along, across from the emblematic Torre de la Giraldilla, is the bastion of the Puerta (Gate) de Sevilla. Built by Iberians, Carthaginians, Romans, Arabs and Christians, it stands witness to Carmona's deep roots and serves as the entrance to the walled city. In its interior, the narrow cobbled streets and whitewashed walls trace a charming and tranquil route past the cathedral-like church of Santa María, the cloistered convent of Santa Clara, with its high trellises, and palaces such as that of the Marques de la Torres, site of the City Museum. It finally reaches the Alcázar de Arriba, the parador (typically 4 or 5 star, historic state-

Carmona. Church of San Pedro (above). ▲
Carmona. Roman Necropolis. Tomb of the Elephant (below).
Carmona. Patio de los Aljibes, Alcázar de la Puerta de Sevilla (above). ▶
Carmona. Roman Necropolis (below).

owned hotels) and the puerta de Córdoba, which offers a panoramic view of the surrounding countryside.

Écija is nestled in the lap of the valley on the banks of the Genil River. Its horizon bristling with belfries, the city has been nicknamed the "city of towers", and its artistic quality is evidenced by the city's urban framework.

The intricate maze of streets surrounding the plaza de España have a number of exuberant Baroque buildings. Palaces such as that of Peñaflor or Benamejí, currently the local museum, are among the finest noble houses in Andalusia, while the churches of Santa Maria, Santiago, Santa Cruz, San Juan and San Gil (with their bright towers made of brick and *azulejos*), compile an excellent collection of architecture, retables, sculptures, paintings and precious metal work.

Between subtle hills are the towns of Marchena – known for its Arab walls and the church of San Juan Bautista, with its collection of paintings by Zurbarán, and other worthy pieces – and Osuna, at the foot of a hill with the remains of an Iberian fortress, with Renaissance silhouettes of the University and Collegiate Church, whose patrimony includes various oil paintings by José Ribera. In the hill's lower reaches, the profusion of residential palaces such as that of the Marques de la Gomera, and the religious and civil buildings, make Osuna a model of noble elegance with an atmosphere that seems to be stuck between the 16th and 18th centuries when it was known as a ducal village.

Sierra Norte of Seville (Sierra Norte Mountains)

The mountains and meadows of the Sierra Norte sharply contrast with the plains that dominate the majority of the province. A change of scenery. Cazalla de la Sierra and Constantina mark the head of this region, both with vestiges of Arab walls, interesting buildings including parishes, convents, and ancestral homes, not to mention fantastic pork products, liquors, and anises. Nearby is the 165,000 hectare extension of the Sierra Norte Natural Park, a protected area significant for the richness of its Mediterranean pine, chestnut and oak forests. It creates an attractive fringe running along the foothills of the Sierra Morena Mountains with a spattering of charming towns such as Alanis, San Nicolás del Puerto, Guadalcanal, etc. and suggestive sights like the ancient monastery of the Cartuja de Cazalla, hidden between springs and groves of trees, the waterfalls and leafy trees of the Huéznar riverbank, and the fantastic limestone landscape hollowed out by erosion and mining from Cerro del Hierro (Iron Hill).

Guadalcanal. Church of the Asunción (above). ▲
Écija (below).
Marchena. Arco (arch) de la Rosa (above). ▶
Collegiate Church of Osuna (below).

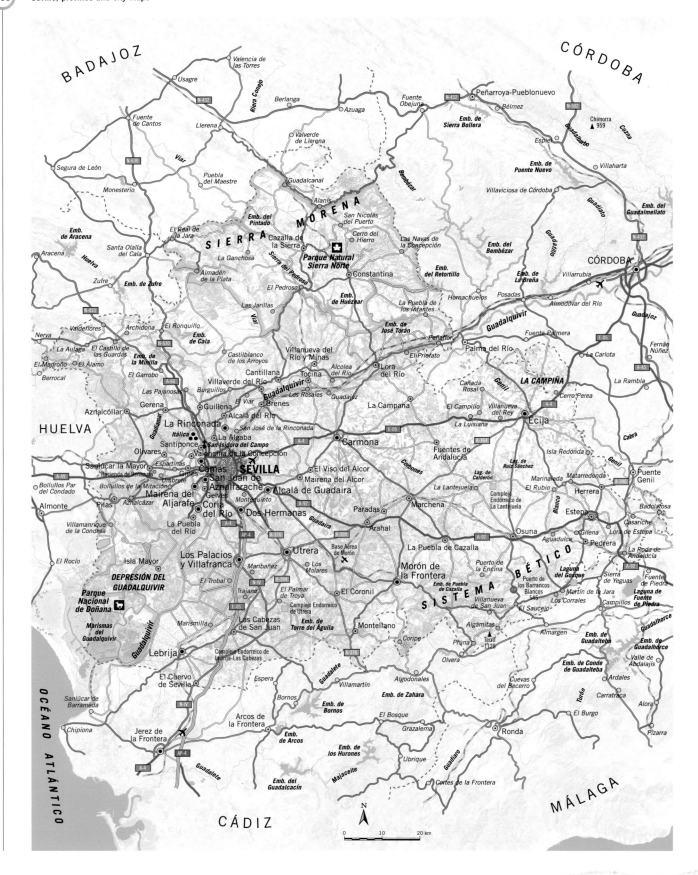

We would like to acknowledge the collaboration of all entities and people who have made this edition possible.

Published by: Ediciones Aldeasa
Editorial Coordination: Carmen de Francisco

Text: Fernando Olmedo
Translation from Spanish: Adrienne Smith
Photographs:
Cover photograph: José Barea
Archivo Ediciones Aldeasa: pages 10-11, 8a, 9, 12-13, 14b, 20, 22-23, 24-25, 26a, 26b, 27, 28a, 28b, 29, 30, 31, 34, 36a, 36b, 37, 38a, 38b, 39, 40, 42, 43, 45, 58a, 58b, 59, 60a, 60b, 61a, 61b, 64a, 65.
José Barea: pages 2, 8b, 15a, 15b, 16a, 17, 18a, 18b, 19, 21, 32a, 35, 48b, 49, 50a, 51b, 54, 55, 56a, 56b, 57, 62c, 63, 64b, 66a, 66c, 67, 71, 72a, 72b, 73, 74b, 75, 77a, 79, 80-81, 82a, 82b, 83, 88-89, 90a, 91, 92a, 94-95, 98 and 99.
Hidalgo-Lopesino: pages 4-5, 6, 14a, 16b, 32b, 33, 44, 46-47, 48a, 50b, 51a, 52-53, 62a, 62b, 66b, 68-69, 70, 74a, 76a, 76b, 77b, 78a, 78b, 84-85, 86, 87, 90b, 92b, 93, 96a, 100-101, 102, 103, 106a, 106b, 107a and 107b.
César Justel: pages 104, 105, 108a, 108b, 109a and 109b.
Iberimage: pages 7, 96b and 97.
Miguel Ángel Nistal Espinoza: page 41.

Graphic Design: Estudio OdZ
Layout: Mariana Grekoff
Cartography: Pedro Monzo
Typeset: Cromotex
Printed by: Gráficas Palermo

© Ediciones Aldeasa, 2006
© of the photographs: Archivo Ediciones Aldeasa
ISBN: 84-8003-513-7
ISBN: 978-84-8003-513-2
Depósito Legal: M-2545-2006
Printed in Spain